off-kilter

off-kilter

Stephanie Conn

Doire Press

First published in 2022

Doire Press
Aille, Inverin
Co. Galway
www.doirepress.com

Layout: Lisa Frank
Cover design: Tríona Walsh
Cover art: artshock @ shutterstock.com
Author photo: Johnny Conn

Printed by Clódóirí CL
Casla, Co. na Gaillimhe

ISBN 978-1-907682-87-2

We gratefully acknowledge the assistance of The Arts Council of Northern Ireland.

LOTTERY FUNDED

CONTENTS

III.

IV.

V.

for Kathy and Helen

INTRODUCTION

We all live busy lives. In 2013, I was spinning many plates—working as a primary school teacher, studying for my MA, raising a young family—then the plates crashed to the ground. For six months, I was confined to bed and could barely lift my head off a pillow. A year of investigations saw me visit one hospital department after another, as medical professionals attempted to join the dots, but failed to. At such times, one's own sanity comes into question as the body refuses to reveal its mysterious secrets. I was eventually diagnosed with the debilitating, chronic, largely invisible, and often contested condition, Fibromyalgia. I had never heard of it.

My life changed completely. I couldn't fulfil many of my previous roles and responsibilities, which left me feeling guilty and stripped of my identity. The question of blame raised its head—was I responsible for what was happening to me? There seemed an endless list of things

I could no longer do—but I could still write. However, I actively kept illness out of my poetry. Writing provided a welcome respite from the daily reality of living with a chronic condition. In 2017, my illness experiences began to make their way onto the page, and in 2018, I undertook a PhD by Practice and began the formal process of writing a poetry collection inspired by chronic illness.

off-kilter is split into five parts, some of which deal with illness directly, others obliquely. The collection sees the body and the environment under pressure; the landscape shifts and burns, the body sickens, relationships fracture. Threat looms large and harsh realities are presented, yet these poems also chart a tentative path through the darkness—animals adapt to hostile conditions, the body rests, and art is created out of the lived experience of chronic illness.

The poems plot a course across the globe from Tasmania in the blistering heat, to Canada and its frozen winter, by way of the Amazon Rainforest and Frida Kahlo's Mexico. Writing out of research into Kahlo's life afforded me, as a writer, a rest from mining the personal experience of illness. A more objective stance is presented, yet one coloured by understanding. It also provided the opportunity to explore illness from a different historical and cultural viewpoint.

Chronic conditions do not just affect the body but infringe on every aspect of a person's life. Illness disrupts, and in the case of chronicity, that disruption is ongoing. In the collection, one subject disrupts another. Each part takes the reader in a different direction, but even within sections disruption features. In part two, for example, a trajectory of the illness narrative builds only to be unexpectedly interrupted by frogs and toads. Likewise, in part five, a family trip provides insight into the long-term management of living with a chronic condition, but these poems are interrupted by ekphrastic poems responding to a range of art works. Similarly, one poetic form disrupts another—a sonnet is followed by a fragmented poem. Fracture exists, but so too does connection, for ideas and images thread through the sections, creating links and parallels, often in unexpected places, and generating echoes throughout.

The collection is arranged to structurally and thematically reflect the complexity of chronic illness. It does not present a single perspective on illness. Rather, diverse, multi-layered, and sometimes contradictory perspectives, take account of the challenges and uncertainties chronic illness presents. Illness actively challenges narrative coherence and any form of literary representation must make room for the chaos it so often enacts. These poems register disturbance, tolerate the unknown and resist closure, as chronic illness demands. In doing so, however, they make room for ambiguity and contradiction, for openness and possibility.

Stephanie Conn
March, 2022

An African Forest Elephant Approaches

1.

When she finally arrives, there's no denying her.
Even this smaller forest kind
is one of the largest mammals on earth.

Other creatures keep their distance.
Know, if they are to eat, they must target
the calf, risk the mother's pointed rage.

Keystone species, uprooting trees, scrub,
turning the savannah to grassland.
In drought they dig, make waterholes.

I creep with all the forest animals,
rest my bare knees on dusty ground,
slake my thirst. My thinning face reflects

sunken eyes. The corners of my mouth
twitch. When I pull back the upper lip
my incisors are growing into tusks.

2.

Now I keep close to water,
protect skin with mud and dust,
walk, don't trot, gallop or jump,
eat for three-quarters of the day —
wrinkles retain water, keep me cool.
I let my pillar legs take the weight,
communicate through seismic signals,
detect vibration in the bones.

I

Cataract Gorge

I've taken both routes to the bridge,
gripped this red suspended metal twice.

Summer. A tan deepening at my neck.
I watched the spot where three rivers meet,
walked the dust track in sandals, turned my back
against dolerite and pressed my stomach
flat when the trail narrowed to a rope.

I heard the click-clack racket of a hundred beetles,
hanging from the tips of trees, disguised as death-
black pussy willow. Laughter bubbled in the throats
of children on swings and leggy teens dived off
a basalt ledge to break the surface of the South Esk.

Spring. These cultivated Victorian gardens
should bloom colour and spray parachute seeds
into the warming air but everything's cold, sodden.
Paths are slipping out of place. Ferns fluoresce
as if they've sucked up the sun's radiating flare.

Rainwater orbs cling to each leafy frond.
The swings have been swallowed by the swell —
a muddy torrent, frothing and foaming at the mouth.
The peacocks take cover under the café awning,
their eyed feathers laid low beside a Coca-Cola sign.

If I'm here again, I'll glide above the basin in a silver
chair-lift, step off by the Japanese Maple, the English Oak.

In the Pleasure Garden

The hens are tired of my flashy strut, have grown accustomed
to my piercing cry. It catches you unaware, turns your head.
What do they know, with their dull plume? You're better dressed.
It's almost ritual, this click and flash from the small, black box
hanging round your neck. I am vibrant. Capture this. Follow
the tease of my tail on the grass, watch it rise, see how it fans.
I ask — have you ever seen such splendour? Draw near, get close
enough to frame each elongated covert quill, my shining crest.
Look to the roof. I will fly for you, display my iridescent brilliance.
I'll not admit my feathers are pigmented brown. Thank heavens
I've been blessed with microscopic make-up that reflects the light,
so I shimmer teal, blue, turquoise, green. You would never guess
and if you do, I'll shift the angle you perceive. It's not deceit.
Don't leave, I'll shake my glorious wings, rattle my tail. Stay!
I'll sing for you, bring you fruit from the forest, deliver it straight
from my beak to your open hand. Stroke my cheek. I am not vain,
just starved of love or stuffed for a king. Don't fear the eyes I drop,
they are extravagant, yes, but harmless. I cannot read your mind —
your thoughts belong to you but let's agree, I truly am a beauty.

Sharing Lunch in Sydney

On the foreshore of Blackwattle Bay in Pyremont —
a fish-market. More than a hundred species laid out
on fold-away tables, a familiar dull against the new,
the coloured flesh, the names we can't pronounce.
We order too much. Watch them slice our catch,
lift it onto steel trays with silver tongs, let it slip
into the pan. We pay. Thank our fishmonger chef.
We rush to taste these strange delights, gaping for air
between bites. We eat from each other's plates,
laugh with full mouths, sip Sauvignon Blanc.
We are ill-disciplined, the subtle flavours merge.

Diving for Snails

Off the east coast of Bruny Island,
neck to toe in neoprene, a man rolls
backwards from the boat's flaked rim,
barely a splash as his body enters water.
Final glimpse of blue flipper and he's gone,
leaving a yellow line slithering on the surface.

Below, he skirts the ragged crevices, pushes
aside seaweed and with a deft flick of the knife
frees a single abalone, big as his hand, from rock,
and shoves it deep into the net tied around his waist.
When it's full he untangles himself from the catch,
tugs the line, sends it up to be counted, weighed.

Later, he offers me the shallow ear-shaped shell,
its lining brilliantly iridescent, shining silver
in the sun, exterior a streaked and mottled
green. He points to the black-edged foot
to indicate the name *Blacklip* but other
words stick in my throat: *gastropod,*
edible, mollusc — I fling it back in.

Delicacy

Pound the dense white flesh.
Place each slice on the hot rack.
Barbecue gently.

Sweet mouthful
of mutton fish.
Tender. Good fortune.

Heat. One hundred days —
the water temperature rising.
All the snails are dead.

Bushfire

There is one road in and out —
mountain to sea and back again.
We take it while we still can,
trail the steady line of traffic
climbing towards a choked sky.

Streams only travel in one direction
or dry up in heatwaves such as this.
The temperatures are still rising.
Last night, as the children slept,
we watched light streak across the sky

illuminating our shack on the hill —
the back steps built close
to jagged shrubs and grass.
This morning we packed everything
and left, shoved pink flip-flops

and beach-balls into the boot,
headed north. We saw flames
above the trees. By nightfall
that road was blistered, nothing
but a scorched leaf-littered underpass,

a net for fiery embers and sparks.
Burning strips of eucalypt bark
leapt from one side of the black lake
to the other. We watch the news,
recognise place names on digital maps

not meant for tourists. We walked
those beaches where huge groups
gather, waiting for the ferocious fires
to burn themselves out, return again
to ash-dusted patches of land.

Bargaining

When life comes down to a headspace of air
beneath a jetty — the atmosphere toxic —
and above, swirling tornadoes of fire,
the house burning down to the ground,
trees glowing scarlet in the haze, hissing,
spitting out sparks, and a fireball sun
beaming yellow, eucalypts exploding
under a Mercurian, orange-streaked sky —
you cling to wood, cling to your grandchildren,
let the youngest lock fingers around your neck,
her blonde curls bobbing on the cold surface,
her eyes wide, lips a thin pale line — you wonder
where their mother is, if she's praying, check
for five heads above water. Make your case.

Tasmanian Tiger

Spotting you from behind, I recognise
the rolling swagger of that awkward gait,
your striped hindquarters, long stiff tail.

You are leaving. A carcass of a bandicoot
lies disembowelled in the dust; a pig-rat
licked clean of blood, tiny ribs gleaming.

Your young suckle out of sight, buried deep
in your pouched belly. Two precious coins,
small, but solid as gold in a furred purse.

Men once paid a pound for your dead frame,
less for your babies and their bolder stripes,
bundled into a bounty-hunter's hessian sack.

I know you can't retract your claws anymore
than they can. When you balanced on hind legs,
stood up to face their barrelled guns, presented

a gaping yawn, did a low growl slip
from your throat? Did you hear the bullet slice
the air, scent poison on the wind, feel the metal

snare your raised heel? It was your prints
that led me into this dry eucalypt forest, three
distinct lobes on the soft pad, so unlike a dog's.

I held your sister's skull in my right hand,
ran my fingers round holes in the palate bone,
watched her pace a screen in black and white.

It's eighty years since she died in a cage.
You seem content here among the blue trees
turning your split gut towards a blazing sun.

Mob

Bush meat requires a clean shot to the skull.
Wallabies, thick as a flock of sheep, graze
on spring crops. A switch flicks, the headlights
stun the night-feeders — steady hand, instant kill.
The body is small and stocky, the hind legs short,
the flesh, muscle tough, is hung to tenderise.

Lean-green, free-range, the father smirks. *Now eat!*
They use their forks to push the steaks
around the patterned plates. *Snivelling pests.*
Farmers in training, they eye their mother,
sniff. They've studied the herbivores at school,
know they use their tails for balance, support.

Swamp-Dweller

More like a herd of cows or belching bulls
than Growling Frogs but these bright green bodies
leapt from the grey swamp, all flailing hind legs
and splayed toes; the gold paint splats on their backs
glinting in the Bass Strait light.
                                    From open
water, the same repeated call, gurgling,
guttural — a warted male, precious
emerald, basking in the sun.
                                    Look beneath
the almost grin — a pale, yellow line, thin,
underlined in bronze, nostril to eye edge,
running the full length of the hunkered
squat to the groin.
                        It's breeding season,
he's growing dark at the throat,
sprouting spiked nuptial pads
on his unwebbed thumbs.

II

Dizzy Spell

To momentarily lose your balance
on the way to the bathroom late at night,
is not that unusual, just drunk on sleep,
staggering naked along the landing,
the walls close enough to keep you upright,

and headaches are common things, though they throb
drowning drumbeats in your skull, make teeth ache.

If I close my eyes in a blacked-out room
and keep my weighted body flat, head sunk
in a breath-stale pillow, this too will pass.
If I swallow the yellow pill four-hourly,
ignore the pinprick smarting of my skin,

I'll step from the bed when a week has passed,
won't crumple, all feeling gone, to the floor.

Under the Skin

There is nothing to see here.
No dislodged bumper battered out of shape,
no shattered windscreen, spray of glass.
There are no body parts, no twisted limbs,
not even blood. The road is dry and clean.
No-one is pacing with a phone or crying.
No-one is taking notes, taking pictures, taking care.
No-one is measuring distance. There is no recovery truck.
The single line of traffic has barely slowed.
There is nothing to see here.

Just a patch of coned-off tarmac
where the cars collided.

Desert Adaptations

I burrow into the stale green duvet,
cover my eyes and ears with gathered down.
I sweat, kick at the weight of feathers,
feel the sheet creep and curl beneath my back,
turn, settle, twist, breathe, sleep —

dream of the water-holding frog
buried beneath sand to stay cool,
secreting mucus from its flat body
to form a thin, crisp cocoon,

until an ochred hand digs deep,
shovels the sleeping frog from its bed,
squeezes it gently, releases the water
stored in groggy organs and pockets of skin.

Post-Collapse

I've been to A&E before —

a foetus dripping from my womb

another, grown almost full, her heart
beating a high-pitched erratic rhythm

another, gone suddenly still
out of trickery

and later, when my babies got sick
        with raging fevers and rashes,
threatened broken bones, struggling lungs

but never alone.

                Never on my own
behind a blue concertina curtain
without a tiny person to focus on.

                Never hearing
drunks slurring obscenities
instead of my children's heartbeats,
breaths, their hushed questions.

                        Never
without their little hands in mine, steeling
myself against what might come next.

I have turned to putty on a plastic bed,
all backbone gone, and when   a floating face
says   *tumour, stroke*   there is nothing

to hold.

Component Part

When he appears between the curtain folds
of my designated square, in his starched coat,
I try to lift my head.

He lowers the bed, bolsters me
on regulation pillows, does not smile,
keeps commands simple.

Follow my pen with your eyes.

I pass the test.

Squeeze my hand.

The right fails.

Try harder.

My throat dries.

Push hard against my palm.

I will remembered strength

but fail over and over
and when he knocks each knee
with his small hammer

the right refuses to budge.
The strip light is blinding.
Bile bubbles from my stomach's pit.

Abbreviations

I sounded out the word. Wrote it neatly.
Ruled a margin in red. I remember the Ps best —
Post Office, postscript, please turn over.

Later, I learned the meaning of those fancy letters
I'd seen inscribed on birthday card invitations: R.S.V.P.
French, no less. *Répondez s'il vous plaît.*

Answer me, please.
My education continues in sterile rooms —
I.V. C.T. M.R.I. I.C.U.

The Brain Ward

We are three —

      the lady in an orthopaedic leather chair
      that props her head up straight
      and holds in place a feeding tube

      the lady who has been revived
      twice — crash cart trailed at speed
      jolted from sleep until *We've got her!*

— and me.

This Week

I drink tea from a straw,
sleep between raised rails,
answer clip-board questions, three times a day:
What is the date? The children's names?
Count to ten and back again.
I pee into a catheter.

Toxicology Report

A frog hops into the ward, approaches me in a tiny white coat,
springs onto the bed, says he's the consultant, gives a wink,
introduces himself with a croak, *xm3jih)hg8f#ga6h!jg2j*gf9du.*

I feed him dry crackers, tell him I've been painting cherry-blossom
petals onto cushioned stones and planting purple daisies in a pot,
when I'm not plucking my eyebrows with a walrus tongue.

He wonders if my head has always been full of sweetie mice,
and if their fur is white or grey or pink, and if the claws
hurt when they draw blood. He taps my veins with webbed

fingers, hoping to turn faint green to blue. He closes
his eyes, presses for the bounce, tells me he is imagining
the layer of skin removed, trusting the route back to the heart.

He hides the bruising with pond weed and tape. Whispers,
best not mention this to anyone. Outside the castle window,
hundreds of bats flap a neurotic dance under a gothic moon.

Cross-Section with Contrast

They are scanning the inside of my body —
abdominal cavity, blood vessels, bones.
Iodine pulses through my veins, flushes warm
and wet between my legs. I've been forewarned,
assured I will not piss myself. A man with kind eyes
squeezes my hand, twice, then steps behind a screen.
I wonder if it's bullet proof. I'm on my back, stripped
of my wedding ring, the necklace from my daughters;
they hold no traction here, in this room of machines
that ignore the heart in favour of the stiller organs.

Trace

When I disappeared, Easter had passed.
My right side vanished first, lost form
and feeling early on; less phantom limb,
more absent hand, foot, arm, leg.

Hadn't parts of me always been coming
and going, fading in certain light,
becoming whole in darkened rooms?

I could not think outside the box
that was a bed, could not raise my half
a head, but placed a map above my face
to wonder where I might have gone.

I followed contour lines with my eye.
Others joined the search but left
the ditches and long grass alone.

There are moments, late at night,
when I'm glad I am no longer here,
except my lung still fills with air;
lifts inside a magician's hat.

Carroting

The hatter told me how he treated beaver skins
with a solution of mercury that turned
the skin-edge orange when it was oven-dried.
How he stretched the pelt to cut thin shreds,
blew the fur into a cone-shaped colander,
added water, passed it through the wet roller
that caused the fur to felt, then peeled free
the loose hood ready to be dyed and blocked.

For a city girl who shuffled papers on a walnut desk,
his story sparkled amber. When we met
in the bar that cold, first night, he was not mad.
When he shook my hand, his fingers didn't shake;
there was no limpness in the wrist and his eyes
met mine without a blink. But the signs were there
in my own fickle heartbeat, in the quarter-smile,
and lodged beneath my nails as gold.

Attending to the Wound

1. Lick the wound

Licking a wound can promote healing.
Let the saliva coat the skin. Its natural
antibacterial agents will do it the world
of good.

2. Do not lick the wound

Licking a wound is unsafe. Saliva
contains a wide variety of bacteria.
The wound could become infected.
Amputation may be required.

A Box of Frogs

Here are the frogs in their carved box,
gathered from four corners of the globe,
croaking close to my ear on the nightstand.
Don't believe the facts, they come alive at dark.

The Glass Frog clinging to plants and trees
in cloud forests, translucent skin, a window
to the pulsing lungs, stomach, pounding heart.

The Tomato Frog, a bounding blood-red drop
against bark, terrific shock of crimson, secreting
toxic gum to make the eyes smart, sting, close.

The Turtle Frog, all flat limbs, beady eyes
and blunt snout, gobbling down termites
having burrowed into their domed hills.

The Poison Dart Frog, sweating out death,
ticking time-bomb, small as a thumb,
flashing striking warnings in greens and reds.

To live, they must keep close to the mind's lake,
absorb my body's moisture. My tear-ducts
are drying out, my skin is puffing up in arid rifts.
The fat frogs spring, slap their skulls off the lid.

III

What I Learned in Winter

1

My tummy rumbles as we pull into the driveway.
Daddy fiddles with his keys, unlocks the door
that is never locked. I shiver, reach a hand into the dark.

He switches on the big light in the living room,
floods the empty space. The room has been stripped
bare of colour — the foil snowflakes falling

from ceiling corners, and the cards draped on string
have gone. The tree has disappeared. Our handmade
decorations — painted Dairylea packs, glittered lolly sticks,

knitted baubles — are wrapped in kitchen roll and shoved
in a box. The little reindeer is flat, all her air let out,
the antlers flop on her red nose. My chest hurts.

2

I like the shape of Dairylea triangles
and the folded silver foil but not
the gloopy cheese between my teeth.
The week before we made our decorations
I had to eat six triangles so it wasn't a waste.

3

Big sisters look after little sisters,
especially when they are only six
and big sisters are already eight.

I know to hold my sister's hand tight
and it feels grown up to walk up the hill
beside the busy road to uncle's house.

The kitchen is cold and I'd like
a biscuit too but tell my sister
to drink her milk and not to cry.

I pull silly shapes with my face
to make her laugh. I see a football
in the garden. I wish the cat would wake.

4

Our cat Casper isn't eating her dinner.
Daddy thinks she knows.
He lets her sleep on his bed.

5

When mummy comes back home
there is less of her, but they have left
her hair and her smile. She shows us
where the doctor used a blue marker
on her skin before he cut the bad bit out.
I close my bedroom door, find a blue felt-tip
in the pencil case I got from Santa
and draw a thick circle round my nipple.

Valance

She kicks a hole in the base of her bed,
drives the petal valance through with her boot,
a livid thrust, enough to make a space
to hide her secrets in — a locked red book,
letters scribbled in invisible ink,
a tissue balled up tight and slipped behind
the wooden slats that hold her when she sleeps
and drop her when she dreams. Two wisdom teeth
jangle in her mouth. She shakes with being
right. The handsome dentist pulls, hauls them out,
says the bleeding will soon stop, plugs the gap
with cotton wool. The waste bin drips bloodied
rags for days. The wound may need a stitch.
She knows a hand has pried beneath her sheets.

Fever

It was glandular. I lay on Matron's daybed
for an hour every afternoon for weeks.
It wasn't the fifties or a Mallory Towers story
but I rested on a floral top sheet staring at her back
as she pretended to write in a thick, black book.

If the door knocked, she would jump to block
my view with a grubby screen. I could hear
every word, no matter how quiet or pathetic —
headaches, sprained ankles, stomach cramps.
It was easy to spot the liars. She knew too.

Once, I gave up my allocated space
to a peaky prefect and returned to class.
The virus lingered, kept me pale, forced
me into bed for months, shapes shifting above
my head, spiders on my skin, spleen fit to burst.

Some called it the kissing disease, evidence
planted as white dots inside my mouth.
At the end of term, Matron said goodbye
but did not wish me well. When I stood
to leave, she gave my hand a single shake.

Breath Work

You breathe deeply to keep the frog calm. Distressed, it will sweat
a concoction of alkaloids into your fattiest organ, leak toxins
to block the transmission of nerve signals. You still rate movement,
are determined to walk beside your daughters a while longer.

For years you've kept coloured tablets out of reach, blister packs
pushed back on the highest shelf, but the frog keeps a stock
embedded in its skin and if the pressure builds, the glands release
their poison. Your perfume bottle has gathered dust, its scent stings.

Everything you eat tastes bitter. You smell burning in the morning.
Hallucinations cast reels of flickering footage across walls —
weddings, new-born babies, unfamiliar living rooms and gardens.
You are there in an ornamental pond, unscrolling your sticky tongue.

On Waking

There are no gods.

I do not seek you out in some twisted underworld
of mist and shadow where deities go undisputed.

I walk on cold ground.

Myth brings such little comfort to the powerless.
I draw on a cigarette, back pressed to pebbledash.

It flickers, sputters smoke.

She had her day. Married in silk, in late summer;
high neck, sheer overcoat. Plucked the memory

for more than twenty years. She had the marriage,
mortgage, home. Birthed three wriggling children;

two healthy girls survived.

Still, she was glad of him; the three years of a tiny
hand in hers, never begrudged her daughters' smiles.

Love was not enough to save either one. Cut off
five days past forty-five is much too young, too much

to bear. I confess I tried.

They said this country had been rid of snakes, choked
up on the venom I would have sucked from her chest.

They lied. I did descend

into a certain kind of dark and found her in a slumberworld,
alive, tight-lipped, nonchalant on the periphery. Daylight —

you are gone all over again.

Gastric Brooding Frogs

The day I swallowed my children
was the day the world took notice.
It was nineteen seventy-four, though
I had been making my stomach a womb
for years, and my mother and her mother
ate their own eggs and felt the alkaline kick
as the hydrochloric acid stopped, a necessary halt
to prevent us digesting our young. I tolerate the fast
when twenty squirming tadpoles hatch in my belly
and wriggle sticky mucus from their gills to keep
the furious acid at bay. My middle bloats until
both my lungs collapse and I must breathe
through my skin till the birthing starts;
propulsive vomiting as I spew out
into the world fully formed young.

Mothering

My child cried to see the toad
splattered on the narrow track.
I didn't know it was the Pipa Toad,
could not comfort with words,
so hugged her tight, believing
the creature dead —
the victim of a wide tyre.
The static amphibian gave no clue
to its *world's flattest* status
until we turned towards the car
and off she hopped —
her back honeycombed
where her mate had stuck
their six laid eggs, intact,
and she had sprouted pouches
to tease out tadpoles.

Failure to Heal

Perhaps the damage was done in heels —
pressure bearing down on the ankle.

Too many strobe-lit, smoky nights,
red-stiletto nights, smudged lips.

Dance floors line-scraped, pock-marked,
eyes bright, chins tilted, cocksure.

Etymology

I heed the O.T., the assigned counsellor,
use approved techniques to challenge blame
but every ancient language points the finger —
assures me pain equals punishment,
retribution; that I must pay, atone.

IV

The Accident

One block south-west from the centre of the universe,
a young couple hurry off a bus to look for her small umbrella
in the square. Empty-handed they board another bus,
Xochimilco bound. She sits by the handrail, reminds herself
of the chocolate and the beautiful new bolero she still has.
Besides, it doesn't look like rain and the sun has lowered
in the sky. Its angle stretches light across an old man's glowing
fingertips, nipping the neck of a brown paper package.

The impact can't have been gentle or silent, leaving her
naked and bloodied, as it did, her body impaled on the rail,
her foot crushed to pulp, her leg fractured in eleven places.
Time did seem to stop, to gather gold dust in a sacred cloud
above her sticky skin, before it cloaked her, making her art,
in the moment before the sirens, screams, cutting, pain.

Mexico City Tracks

I knew all about the black funeral trams carrying
ninety percent of the city's deceased to the cemetery,

and ancient human sacrifices stretched over stone
so the priest could rip out the heart, cut off the head,

fling what remained of the dead down the pyramid steps.
I was thinking of neither when the tram flung me forward,

crushed me completely. I was longing for my coloured bolero,
the shining box of it, how it opened at the chest, and as metal

pierced my flesh like a panther's tooth, cut between
my legs, I saw only bright shades — red, violet, gold.

Broken from the inside out: spinal cord, collar bone,
pelvis, ribs; robbed of my virginity by an iron rod,

I should have died. They sewed me back together
on a folding table. I should have died. I lived —

and as my head was still intact, they placed
a mirror above so I could feast on my face.

Pata de Pelo

At six years old pull four socks up the shin
of the thin leg they wash in walnut water,
rub gently with small, hot towels. Father,
grown tender, tells you run, skate, box, swim, kick.
You cycle like a demon child round the park,
row Chapultepec Lake, flash black bloomers
climbing trees, hurl curses when they call you
peg-leg, tell your imagined friend their names.
At twenty-six, perfect the swish and swirl
of flowing A-line skirts, trimmed with pleated lace.
Clutter your neck with starched frills, silk ribbons,
sling jade and fire opals from gold chains.
Gather your hair in dark, flamboyant knots,
braid in place with clips and orchid blooms.
Present a bold stare that dares any living soul
to look away or look lower, deeper,
to see the withered leg, the limp, the back brace
reinforced with metal bars, leather straps,
the plaster casts: your moulded second skin.

Xenopus Test

In a lab full of urine and toads,
technicians fill each syringe to the line.

The small glass jars, not smashed in the post,
are laid out in sickly rows of pale piss.

Lifted, one by one, from the tank
by a gloved hand, the African Clawed Toads

extend their plump thighs to the needle,
are popped back into the metal chamber.

Results come quickly. Hundreds of empty eggs.
Now is the time of deep breaths and belief.

Lower your eyes from the full moon,
lay a silver necklace across the collar bone

to deflect the ghostly rays —
place a dagger under your bed.

By Mouth

Knowing my body to be brittle,
I visit the doctor in the fourth week
for a longhand script.

It fails to abort —
and I allow myself to think
this might be the baby to thrive.

Each night I cramp a little more,
and in the morning, everything
tastes bitter.

Gathering Bark

I dream of the evergreen Cinchona tree,
her fruit, a capsule brimming with seeds,
her flowers, tubular, pink, rose, red —
beneath a shock of corolla lobes.

At dusk the girdling starts —
the stripping bare of bark in rings,
to dry and quill and grind to dirt.
The fever tree is dying.

At the boundaries of sleep
the forests are disappearing,
loaded ships set sail, and in my palm
a glowing blossom turns to dust.

Doll Collection

My favourite boy doll is Leonardo.
I write his baptism certificate in Art Deco

letters — capitals. I make to-do lists —
appointments at the doll hospital,

the dolls that need a new outfit,
new hair, new body parts.

In their little beds I lay them down to sleep,
kiss each porcelain head, each cold cheek.

Menagerie

My babies are numerous.
They show their love
in purrs and licks and yelps.
Doves, deer, parrots, cats —
my cherished companions
have spirited eyes
that watch and know
my every whim.
I hold my clever creatures
to my chest so they might
hear my heart beating.
The spider monkeys tug
at my breasts like children.
My rare beauties,
the Xoloitzcuintlis,
play in the courtyard
then clamber over my body,
limp in the bed, to feel warmth.
Their hairless bodies thrill me.

Embryo

the doctor has sent me a gift
a foetus in formaldehyde

i set the heavy jar on my desk
in the mornings i like to look closely

i gather bones and organs
as i might gather pebbles petals insect wings

study them under a microscope
or in a thick biology book

the drawings i scrape into metal
are anatomically correct

though i experiment
with scale and perspective

i am of sound mind not drawn
into their sorry superstitions

i cannot believe butterflies carry
the souls of our lost babies

each year on the dia de los myertos
i wait for the monarchs to return

Migrating South

Autumn. East of the Rocky Mountains.
Monarch butterflies note the angle of the light,
a drop in temperature, the senescence of milkweed —

take flight...

All along the Trans-Mexican Volcanic Belt we wait.
Wait for the sound, the soft patter of rain on a dry
afternoon, for a lava cloud to appear overhead.

They cluster on pine and oyamel trees, make them glow.
Under the weight of orange wings, veined with black,
branches droop. The whole forest is quivering.

Gift

He fixed your sculpted butterflies to my night-time sky,
content to have their delicate wings sealed behind glass.

He thought if I saw them just before sleep, I might not
dream of your touch, butterfly soft, and burn in the dark

at the urgent memory of your breath on my neck.
He liked to think them dead and pinned at the heart.

They have such short lives. Oh, but the colour, the glorious
flight — to soar, the scent of orange blossom on your wings.

Casa San Angel

we each live alone
cuboid blocks on raised columns
joined by a concrete bridge

our own studios
his, two-storied, glass-walled, red
mine, smaller, peacock blue

we like to mix, match
wooden tables painted bright
tubular steel chairs

cantilevered steps
much too difficult to climb
lead to a roof terrace

exposed pipes, chimneys
cables draped like spider's web
metal rubbish ducts

in this functional
space, we separate often
make love to others

affluent suburb
west of the city, we live
bordered by cacti

Cocoon

I long to return,
not to the blue house,
but to the warm blanket of my body —
before it turned on itself, failed to grow
my babies whole. I ache to fill my limbs,
feel skin plump, find myself in flesh and bone,
not in silk petals or metal's straight chill
but in the shift of cells and breath and blood.
I want to let my hair hang long and loose,
pluck my eyebrows thin, wax my upper lip,
turn my head from the butterfly's
exquisite flight, sleep — become
a fat caterpillar again.

Framed in Velvet

There are always tears.
A heaving heart lies bleeding on the sand.
The painted sky is a cloudscape.

Arteries pulled taut and tied above two blood-red hangers —

one holds the past — the slight shift of school wear,
white blouse, blue skirt, in a summer-term breeze,
for my younger self — tanner, taller, thinner.

The other, my necessary preference for traditional dress —

the huipil, pulled loose from a backstrap loom,
is the dark shade of dried blood, grown viscous, cool,
a black and gold brocade chain-stitched into place.

My skirt falls in sage folds, is hemmed in lace —

above a club foot, made boat, seaworthy,
if only it were cut, split at the groin.
I straddle land and sea — a black ocean made still.

To the west my Sierra Madre rise above the desert.

The rod, that pierces the place where the heart should be,
glows, holds angels at its see-saw ends, belongs
not in woven threads or pleated silks but in the sky.

That empty space fires the amygdala — a memory of absence.

The heart shudders, pumps rivers of blood
up towards the mountain paths,
leaks a crimson flood, stains the sand rust.

I am closer now, almost close enough to take your arm.

Under a Gangrene Sun

They are coming for my foot —
will cut the leg beneath the knee
to stop the pain, stop the poison spreading.

They've been shooting Demerol into my arm
for months to make the screaming stop,
stabbing deeper into collapsed veins.

My brow softens. Diego lifts his gaze, at last,
to meet my woozy stare and a fire-star
falls to earth, melts into green leaves

on the ward floor, before it turns to desert sand.
Everything is rotten and shifts in a canopy of thorns —
toes swing on stripped branches, hang from beaks.

I hold my peacock ring in my left hand,
a clay deer in my right, try to remember who
brought them, if it was you, sobbing by my bed.

You weren't so sentimental when my heart
shattered, yet you blub for my poor dead foot —
birth red turned to brown, black, then blacker still.

I love you most of all. You give me wings
and I've never needed them more than today
putting on my Tehuana dress to meet the knife.

There was a general Mesoamerican conception of thirteen heavens, and the Maya, at least, pictured these heavens as a profile of a pyramid of seven tiers with one heaven at the top and six along each side.
— John M. Ingham

*I would build my world
which, while I lived,
would be in agreement
with all the worlds.*

*I hope the exit is joyful —
and I hope never to come back.*

— Frida Kahlo

Toads

first heaven — sky where the moon moves

Weathered
but still up-
right, stone
columns
placed in
formation
a history of
ritual in relief
at Izapa. Altars
squat as toads
their faces
broad and flat
eyelids heavy
toxic shoulder
sacks distinct.
Receptacles
on sloping
backs to burn
an offering
open portals
to another
world.

second heaven — where the stars move

At Kaminaljuy —
three miniature toad mortars,
three pestles, unearthed.

third heaven — where the sun moves

Before the curanderos suture wounds with human hair,
set bone, trephine the skull, plug perforated teeth
with jade, turquoise, haematite — they meet in moonlight,

carved shell gorgets hanging from their necks, feathers
quivering above their heads, to lick the sticky ooze
off the pitted parotid glands of the Marine Toad.

A whistle haunts the sky. Three shifting shapes
crouch and spring, perform a choreographed divination.
The scent of salt and aromatic pine rises with flame.

They break the surface of an unseen lake,
swim with water-snakes, uo frogs, fish,
crocodiles — feel their shoulders slump

under the weight of their jaguar heads.
Each incants a question formed of loss,
waits for answers, starts the journey back.

fourth heaven — the sky of the big star

I am seeing double, two of us, almost identical
linked by our hearts' pulmonary vein.
We know not to look each other in the eye
but clasp hands to complete the circuit.

To my right, you are bodiced, a hint
of blue about the lips, high-necked in lace,
tied white bows, blood dripping on your skirt
where scissors have severed the flow.

To your left, I am bra-less, grown rounder,
my edges soft against the dappled sky, natural
under loose fabric, legs spread in rest, back straight.
I've placed my palm below yours to keep us buoyant.

fifth heaven — sky that is sinking

Diego, darling toad,

though I worship willingly, make you
an idol, devote myself in rowdy reverence,

I have yet to work out the portion of you
that proves hallucinogenic and not deadly.

sixth heaven — dark green space

If, like the hero twins, Hunahpu and Xbalanque,
failure runs through the bloodline
(a mother's cancerous cells, a father's jerking fits)
best to swallow it whole. Imagine a louse.

Pass the message silently from body to body —
a toad holds the louse in her bloated belly
waits to be eaten by a snake
that slips down the throat of a hawk

until a whisper from the underworld
announces itself from a hooked beak —
a piercing scream to the sky
and you ready yourself for the task.

seventh heaven — region of blue

I have cut off my hair.
Dark strands litter
the earth like roots
torn at the source.

This suit is too wide
on my wasted shoulders
and the leather shoes pinch
but my head feels lighter.

eighth heaven — where the obsidian knives are creaking

I drive with the doctor
to the city outskirts.

It is spring. He needs
me to be cheerful.

We pass brick kilns,
a sky thick with smoke.

They are burning pine.
Choked air is incense.

I paint trees with bare
branches — black brush

strokes grown imprecise.
A fat man in a sombrero

stokes the last oven
with a long thin stick.
It glows red, turns to cinder,
gathers as ash on our lips.

ninth heaven — region of white

I pray to Chac, to Tlalac, the Virgin, Mother Earth,
these damn walls, to deliver rain, to strike the clouds
or shake rain-snakes to release me from this dry hell.

I'll croak and chant, be a red-eyed frog if I must,
offer a banquet, throw myself down a well —
what more harm could I do to this corpse

I once called body? It's too hot to hold you
against my skin and the drugs make me sweat.
The distance grows. I pray to Tlalac, to Chac...

tenth heaven — region of yellow

Move my bed from this rancid room,
transport me — let me levitate —
towards the light, to glass panes
where I can watch rainfall
conjure swirling puddles,
as pigeons splash
in ceramic pots
half-buried
in pocked
walls.

eleventh heaven — region of red

I spit at the government office limits.
Spineless signatories, what do they know
of my pain, my daily suffering?

But you, dear friend, you understand.
Draw close, hand me my vials, add
another dose of Demerol to the syringe.

No need to check for loose particles,
discolouration. Find a patch of skin
between the scabs and scars —

stick the needle in. When I sleep,
slip out, don't say a word, take
my love into the shadowed street.

twelfth heaven — sky that is the place of the gods

I dream of the Sapodilla tree,
her long and twisting root system,
resistance to wind, delicate cream flowers —
small bells that chime inside my foggy head.

I discard the rough brown skin in leaf-litter
share the sweet-soaked flesh of her fruit
with howler monkeys, a sun-blind kinkajou,
while yellow epauletted bats sip at nectar syrup.

My fingernails sprout claws, slash at bark, slice
the trunk for her milky sap. I know the harvesters
boil and block and cut but I drop to my knees,
let the chicle drip into my mouth until I choke.

thirteenth heaven — place of two

When breath leaves my body,

burn the broken column to dust.

Put what remains in a Mayan jar

of limestone and volcanic ash —

a monochrome tempered toad.

I'll wait inside your hollow heart.

Pigment

Black squirrel, bolshy
on top of a carpark bin —
downtown Toronto.

My city-slicker
cousin tuts — *dirty rodent* —
as I take a snap.

Are you mad? Brows raised.
Why would you photograph that?
She cannot believe

I've not seen its kind,
and no, she doesn't know why
they are black, or here.

I do my research,
learn that it is a mutant —
quirk of DNA,

exactly the same
species as the common grey.
The pigment gene fails —

a single hormone
turns the colour switch to off —
jet black hair grows thick,

conserves precious heat,
thermal gain in bitter cold,
they surge northwards.

Active and outdoors
the long, freezing winter months,
they leap, tumble, thrive;

scamper in backyards,
city-parks, hang out in bare
trees and parking lots.

I'm the intruder,
shivering in fur-lined boots,
layers stuffed with down.

At night I stretch, turn,
ache, try hard to visualise
a knotted nucleotide.

Travelling North

Huge glaciers, twelve thousand years ago,
advanced then retreated to form this land;
these mixed wood plains of South Ontario.
Our kids roll their eyes in the back, raise hands
to shove in earphones and drown out the sound
of your researched facts. We drive through Uxbridge,
startle a white-tailed deer on Chalk Lake Road,
and I feel strangely at one with Oak Ridge
Moraine, having too been hollowed out, scraped,
prodded, in the name of moving forward;
a glacial shift in the dark, cause unknown.
No-one mentioned ice. This frozen landscape
of rolling hills and valleys suits my mood.
I'm glad to be four thousand miles from home.

Caldera

...there was blood and tongues of fire above the blue-black fjord...
and I sensed an infinite scream passing through nature.
                                        — Edvard Munch, 22 January 1892

When crossing the bridge above the fjord,
consider your proximity to the slaughterhouse
and Utsikten lunatic asylum, as you look
to the scorched sky. At this northern latitude
the heavens bleed nacreous clouds. A year since
Krakatoa lost her head, ripped apart Rakata island.

I collapsed, smoke-laden, and slept in a cauldron's hollow,
dreaming of hands sculpting a purple halo round the star,
sharp-lit diffracted light, ice-crystals shaped into night clouds.
I float above my body and when the feeling doesn't go
they assign a label like *distortion*. Glass keeps us separate,
warps my features, reflects a blue-green moon, scatters ash.

There Are Many Ways to Spear a Fish

The window frames a story of storm;
black cumulonimbus, churning waves,
cracking light. A night for indoors.

The room's lines are distinct. In my dreams
there's always been a lack of edge. I am
awake and watching the world turn outside in.

Moonlight catches the ocean's pleats,
illuminates her hidden veins beneath gilt-
edged clouds. They gather in copper casing.

The thunder is close enough to spark
a pounding in my chest. I do not see
the lightning streak across the sky

but feel it pierce my silver skin, lift me
clean of the tide, exposing my underside
to the crackling air. I am singular,

propelled from the shifting rainbow shoal
where each tilt and turn seems laid down
in my tapered bones, etched in fin and tail.

I gasp once, fail to feel the sea trickle
through my gills. I long to breathe in
the strangeness, fill phantom lungs,

no longer coffined by the endless swell.
I am thrust into a new-fangled, half-lit scene,
staring, with unblinking eyes, at the stars.

Nathan Phillips Square, Toronto

This square is rectangular.
The city's name is spelled out
in colour — three feet high,
twenty-two feet long, before 2016,
when they added the maple leaf.

These 3D LED letters illuminate dusk;
Wi-Fi controlled colour combinations —
twenty-eight million, approximately;
equal to what the eye can see,
although the wind is making it difficult.

The Reflecting Pool has become an ice-rink.
Skates are available to rent by the hour.
The three concrete arches, that hold the rink
in place, have since been named for freedom,
and slid into the base, a piece of the Berlin Wall.

The Nutcracker on Yorkville Avenue

In the wings the dancer waits,
counts herself in from a growing list:
swollen metatarsophalangeal joint,
second metatarsal stress break,
flexor hallucis longus tendinitis
and — smile, toes, leap —

breath quickens. We sit forward in red velvet
seats, follow the swirl of fabric, colour, sheen,
lean towards the melody, the crescendo,
the high delicate chimes of the celesta;
a fountain dripping with pear drops,
the sound once caught on a Paris street.

Backstage, she unwraps her crumpled toes,
warms them with thin fingers, stretches her belly
flat to the floor, packs her bag until tomorrow night.
Filing out, we are breathless still, blood pulsing.
From the glass staircase, everything glitters. Winter's bite
is easier with a busker playing 'White Christmas' to our first snow.

Gold Threads

This lie is your past

tacked together from magazine
clippings, calendars, photo-frame
families and others' dreams.

Their papered gloss is your silk —
enough to stitch intricate gowns
to warm your pallid skin.

It goes as far back as you remember —
this Hall of Mirrors reflects your future
in a glare of blurred technicolour.

Remember the night you grew into a real girl —
inside a striped tent the scent of cinnamon
and spun sugar sweetening the tang of blood,

how you danced inside a kaleidoscope —
pressed together in turns, tulle twisting
at your waist, until you saw stars.

A Tonal Shift in Edge

This is not a watercolour moment
but one that emerged from acid
smeared on copperplate, and cutting,
in the dank corner of a locked room.

When the door opens onto a raging sea,
without the draw of shingle or sand,
do not shrink from this framed space
or let doubt bleed into the architrave.

Close your eyes. Forget all you've been told
about looking and leaping. Taste the ocean
on your lips, and if you desire a soundscape,
pucker to a whistle in the nipping wind.

Become a bird. Let your elongated wings
find the air's current, lift you high above
wood and walls, crashing waves; carry you
from landlocked salt lakes to the open sea.

Branta Canadensis

The temperature drops two days into our trip
and my head won't lift from the pillow
when I try to rise for breakfast.

My husband sticks to the planned itinerary,
eats brunch at my cousin's house,
a split-level, east of Toronto.

No-one mentions the burnt cinnamon toast
or the fact the coffee's bitter, barely warm.
The adults volley catch-up chat,

make arrangements for the following day.
The kids step out onto a fresh fall of snow,
look to the racket in the heaving sky —

a flock of Canada Geese form a perfect V
above their hooded heads. They should be
flying south. They honk and fly north.

Snowtubing on New Year's Day

They walk together through clean snow to reach the lift —
then sit, spread-eagled, in red inflatable rings, to be dragged,
at regular intervals, up the steep incline to the top of the hill.

The youngest, my cousin's child, is seven and safe here.
Slopes for all ages and abilities; fun for the whole family.
My father is seventy and grinning at the camera in a beanie hat.

They take off laughing and twisting, sliding down the lanes
of ploughed snow, cheeks flushed, a babble of eager chatter
as they whoop and holler below a blue, cloudless sky.

They will remember this day for years to come, tummies
flipping somersaults, the bounce of bobble hats, arms linked.
They gather at the bottom, ready themselves for another go.

I've stayed behind, again, beneath a patchwork quilt that hurts
my skin. I watch TV on mute, sip the tepid water within reach,
try to muster enough energy to climb four carpeted stairs.

The Staircase

I have wakened at the bottom of the stairs,
am stripped bare, skin translucent in the dusk light,
a featureless cartoon figure, not yet coloured in.

The staircase is orange and cold underfoot —
I think of terracotta pots, kiln-fired clay, burnt umber,
a desert landscape without a hint of blossom.

I am so much smaller than I recall —
the stairs rise above me at an impossible slant,
each bigger, higher, steeper than the last.

My shadow has grown cruel, misshapen,
leaks large like an ink blot onto the first step,
the one I am still standing on, looking up.

Scoville Scale

Chilli peppers break through his skin
where the body joins piece to piece,
stab and pierce at his shoulders, wrists,
ankles, knees, toes, leak capsicum flesh
like candle wax onto his fissured limbs.

He is beaten, broken, accepting of his fate,
the sharpest knives have grown blunt
in their familiarity — no longer slice or cut
but tear and trail and sting and burn.
Frown lines are carved, deep set.

Eye bags black, skin dull-bruised,
neck grown gaunt, bone rubbed bone,
fiery blasts of self-defence. Birds peck
unperturbed at the chilli seeds, his eyes.
Full, they fly. Abandoned alabaster man.

Snowy Owl

Taking the 401 in the low light
of a December afternoon, the snow
suddenly ceased — revealed a white owl
majestic, on a metal bridge stretched across
the highway, statuesque above the rush
of traffic intent on leaving the city, car
horns pressed, fumes condensed to ghosts.
He is insulated to his black claws
by down, thick feathers, detects his prey
in small movements, reflected sound waves.
Perched high and still, he suggests himself
as ice-sculpture, prepares to launch his hushed
attack into an unseen field, to swallow whole
a deer-mouse, digest the flesh, regurgitate
bones, teeth, quills, fur — the indigestibles.

Hinterland

That night my father's story entered my dream.
The car brought to a halt at a stop light,
a white-tailed deer bounding from snowy woodland
to slip and skid, startled by the early morning ice
and the silver truck on a secluded backroad.
A fawn, she'd lost her fairy-tale white spots,
her fine red coat had turned coarse grey.
She had been nibbling winter forbs and sedges
under cover of cedar and spruce, had not yet
grown scrawny, a gaunt shadow-self, longing
for spring greens. Mid-summer will arrive,
see her red again, grown sleek and sturdy.

I wake to my fortieth birthday, to white
drumlin roofs and the street disappeared.
Soon, neighbours will emerge to shovel drives
and sidewalks, sprinkle salt. The sky's powder blue,
clouds spun sugar, sun bright, but the snow stays put.
This is a dry cold, not the damp, seeping sort of home,
not bone cold. Here, it is enough to wrap up warm
in hats and scarves, slip on boots and go outside.
My body can tolerate this freeze —
feels its age but not the added years.
I brave a sleigh on a small hill, laugh mid-flight,
tumble into a drift without a whimper.

ACKNOWLEDGEMENTS

Acknowledgements are due to the editors of the following publications in which versions of some of these poems first appeared: *Abridged, Anthology of Illness* (Emma Press), *Bangor Literary Journal, Banshee, Coast to Coast, Elbow Room, Empty House: Poetry and Prose on the Climate Crisis* (Doire Press), *Honest Ulsterman, Interpreter's House, Intersections Postgraduate Journal, Iota, Metamorphic* (Recent Works Press), *North, Ofi Press, Poetry Ireland, Poetry Jukebox, Poetry Salz-burg, Southword, Stony Thursday Book, Studi Irlandesi, The Music of What Happens* (New Island Books), *The Paperclip, The Pickled Body, The Tangerine* and *Watch Your Head*.

'Mexico City Tracks' was featured in Poetry Ireland's Poetry Day Truth or Dare resources. 'There Are Many Ways to Spear a Fish' and 'A Tonal Shift in Edge' were featured as part of Belfast Print Workshop Archive's 40th Birthday Creative Writing Project. 'Bushfire' won third prize in the Dromineer Poetry Competition.

Thanks to the Arts Council of Northern Ireland, University of Atypical and Newtownabbey Borough Council for their financial support in completing this collection. Thanks also to Words Ireland, as some of these poems were developed as part of their mentoring programme; to Lisa and John for their continued belief in my work and to Tríona for her work on the cover.

Heartfelt thanks to Kathleen McCracken, Moyra Donaldson, Emma Must, Siobhán Campbell and Frank Sewell for their engagement with these poems, invaluable feedback and encouragement. To Paul Maddern, the gift that is The Rivermill, and to all those I met around its dinner table. To Kathy and Helen, to whom this book is dedicated, for their friendship, support and good times. To Gillian, for everything. And to my long-suffering family, Johnny, Emily and Katie. x

STEPHANIE CONN is a poet and creative writing facilitator and former teacher. Her publications include *The Woman on the Other Side* (Doire Press, 2016), *Copeland's Daughter* (Smith/Doorstop, 2016) and *Island* (Doire Press, 2018). Stephanie is a graduate of the MA programme at the Seamus Heaney Centre, QUB, and the PhD programme at Ulster University. Stephanie's prizes include the Seamus Heaney Award for New Writing, Funeral Service NI Prize, Yeovil Poetry Prize and Poetry Business Pamphlet Competition. *The Woman on the Other Side* was shortlisted for the Strong/Shine Award for Best First Collection. The recipient of a range of arts awards, bursaries and residencies, Stephanie has read her work locally, nationally and internationally.